TIME BELONGS TO GOD AND OTHER POEMS

LEONG KWOK THYE

WESTBOW
PRESS®
A DIVISION OF THOMAS NELSON
& ZONDERVAN

WestBow Press books may be ordered through booksellers or by contacting:

WestBow Press
A Division of Thomas Nelson & Zondervan
1663 Liberty Drive
Bloomington, IN 47403
www.westbowpress.com
1 (866) 928-1240

ISBN: 978-1-9736-0811-0 (sc)
ISBN: 978-1-9736-0812-7 (e)

Library of Congress Control Number: 2017917628

Print information available on the last page.

WestBow Press rev. date: 08/22/2019

Contents

Foreword

"Hurricanes, tsunamis, earthquakes,
The earth in fury shakes!
Millions homeless, families in distress,
Dreams shattered, lives in a mess.
Does God care?"

This is just one of the many stanzas you will find in this inspiring collection of poems. In addition to the heart wrenching theme of "hurricanes, tsunamis and earthquakes", you will also find humorous but helpful analogies in poetic verse, "I have a super mobile phone, That doesn't cost a cent."

But whether heart wrenching or humorous, they are helpful and harnessed to Scripture passages.

I have enjoyed and been edified by these poems and it is a pleasure to recommend this collection. Thank you, Kwok Thye!

Rev. Dr. Gordon Wong
President
Trinity Annual Conference
The Methodist Church in Singapore

Introduction

We live in a complex and chaotic world; a world characterized by uncertainty and insecurity. This collection of poems offers insights from the Bible of problems and challenges that continually confront and often overwhelm us.

The aim is to provoke thinking; to encourage readers to explore the Bible to discover for themselves the reality and relevance of God. We need a change in our attitude towards God. The apostle Paul summarized this succinctly when he told the believers in the church in Rome to be, "transformed by the renewing of your mind. Then you will be able to test and approve what God's will is - his good, pleasing and perfect will." (Romans 12:2)

We have a mighty and loving God who is in control and who cares. Knowing him and enjoying a personal relationship with him offers meaning and fulfillment in life and hope beyond our existence on earth.

Leong Kwok Thye

Author's Note

The First and Second Editions of this collection of poems published by Scripture Union Singapore in 2014 & 2015 used Bible verses from the New King James Version. This Third Edition uses Bible verses from the more reader-friendly New International Version. Minor changes have been made in the lyrics of some poems to enhance clarity of thought and expression.

*26"What good will it be for a man
if he gains the whole world,
yet forfeits his soul?*
Matthew 16:26

*12Teach us to number our days aright,
that we may gain a heart of wisdom.*
Psalm 90:12

Time Belongs To God

We measure life by length of days,
And extend its span by ingenious ways,
But when life will actually end,
Is ultimately in the Creator's hand.

What then should be our goal?
To gain the world and lose the soul?
Or walk with God in humility,
And set our sight on eternity?

God measures life by how we live,
The time to him we give,
By purity of heart,
And the blessings we impart.

Teach us Lord, to number our days,
To think your thoughts and walk your ways,
To gain a heart of wisdom
For the glory of your kingdom.

[10]I denied myself nothing my eyes desired; .....
[11]Yet when I surveyed
all that my hands had done .....
everything was meaningless, ...
a chasing after the wind; .....
Ecclesiastes 2:10,11

Chasing After The Wind

We seek satisfaction
In material treasure,
And gratification
In personal pleasure.

We seek achievements
To gain fame,
And build monuments
To establish our name.

But selfish ambitions
Of every kind
Are mere illusions;
A chasing after the wind.

O God, our Creator, give
Knowledge, joy, and wisdom;
To enable us to live
Your way in your kingdom.

⁶"Seek the Lord while he may be found; .....
⁷Let the wicked forsake his way .....
Let him turn to the Lord, ...
for he will freely pardon.
Isaiah 55:6,7

Seeking God

We seek God - he is missing!
But he has not been hiding -
Our evil thoughts and ways,
Have shielded us from his face.

When we forsake wickedness,
To seek him in his holiness,
Then in mercy he will forgive,
And show us how to live.

For his thoughts are better,
And his ways are higher.
He gives blessings in abundance
To all who heed his guidance.

He makes the rain and snow
Water the earth for plants to grow.
So too when wickedness cease
He will bless us with joy and peace.

¹The heavens declare the glory of God;
the skies proclaim the work of his hands.
³There is no speech or language
where their voice is not heard.
Psalm 19:1,3

Discovering God

The glory of the burning sun
Reflected in the gleaming water,
Declares the majesty of One
Who is Creator and Sustainer.

The waves in the boundless sea
Rolling ceaselessly onto the shore,
Declares God's eternity
Of time past and forevermore.

The countless stars in space
Extending into infinity,
Declares God's wondrous grace
Reaching out to all humanity.

We behold your glory, Lord,
In things that we can see.
Help us through your living Word
To discern your sovereign majesty!

^{30}Even youths grow tired and weary, ...
^{31}but those who hope in the Lord
will renew their strength.
They will soar on wings like eagles;
they will run and not grow weary,
they will walk and not be faint.
Isaiah 40:30,31

Soaring On Eagles' Wings

Amidst challenges and strife,
We run the marathon of life.
Everyone must participate;
How we run decides our fate.

It's an arduous journey;
All will be weak and weary.
Everyone will need strength
To complete the entire length.

But we are not on our own;
The Creator is on the throne.
He gives power to the meek
When they are weary and weak.

Lord, as we wait on you;
Our ebbing strength renew.
Empower us by your grace
To run with steadfast pace.

That dispirited no more,
On eagles' wings we soar
Upward to finish the race,
To see you face to face.

*[31]God saw all that he had made,
and it was very good. .....
Genesis 1:31*

*[21]..... creation itself will be liberated
from its bondage to decay .....
into the glorious freedom
of the children of God.
Romans 8:21*

Does God Care?

Hurricanes, tsunamis, earthquakes,
The earth in fury shakes.
Millions homeless, families in distress,
Dreams shattered, lives in a mess.
Does God care?

God created the earth, it was good;
A beautiful garden with luscious food.
Clear water and pristine skies,
And life with him that never dies.
Did God care?

The earth was for our enjoyment;
We have abused it to our detriment
By our arrogance and greed.
Catastrophes are signs to heed.
Did we care?

Lord, teach us to work with you
To remake the earth anew;
That those who come after
May enjoy your blessings forever.
Will we care?

8"Will a man rob God? .....
10Bring the whole tithe into the storehouse .....
I will ..... pour out so much blessing
that you will not have room enough for it."
Malachi 3:8,10

We Have Robbed God

In a world of plenty,
The coffers of nations are empty.
The rich have less,
The poor remain penniless.

We have robbed God!
With things we shouldn't afford;
Exploited the poor and powerless
By our greed and ruthlessness.

Lord, give us a heart to care,
And a willingness to share.
Replace our selfish obsession
With your love and compassion.

Teach us to give back to you
What is your rightful due.
Accept our tithes and offering,
And pour out your blessing.

¹He who dwells
in the shelter of the Most High
will rest in the shadow of the Almighty.
¹⁴"Because he loves on me …..
¹⁵….. I will …..
¹⁶….. show him my salvation
Psalm 91:1,14-16

God Is Our Refuge

The Most High God is our shelter
From fear, harm and danger.
In the shadow of the Almighty
There is comfort and security.

The Lord saves the unaware
From the fowler's snare.
His faithfulness is guarantee
Of their absolute security.

Multitudes will fall by the way;
But all who call on him will stay,
For his angels protect from harm,
Those under his mighty arm.

Shelter us from storms of life;
Free us from the tyranny of strife.
Grant us peace and serenity
Under your shadow, Lord Almighty.

¹Unless the Lord builds the house,
its builders labour in vain. .....
³Sons are a heritage from the Lord, ...
⁵Blessed is the man
whose quiver is full of them. .....
Psalm 127:1,3,5

⁶Train a child .....
when he is old
he will not turn from it.
Proverbs 22:6

Arrows On Target

Unless God builds the family,
All effort is futility.
Children are a gift from God,
They are our reward.

Like arrows in a quiver,
Will our children deliver?
Are they on target?
Will we live to regret?

Train a child the way to go;
They will surely follow,
If we offer a sample
Of our life as an example.

Lord, build our family,
Guard over our city.
Come into our lives to reign,
Lest we labour in vain.

*37 ..... "The harvest is plentiful
but the workers are few.
Matthew 9:37*

*14How, then, can they call on the
one they have not believed in?.....
Romans 10:14*

Into The Lord's Harvest

God's task for all of us
Who love and follow Jesus;
Is to spread his joyous word
To all who have never heard;
That there is no condemnation
When they accept his salvation.

The task is truly fruitful,
As the harvest is plentiful.
For in every race and creed,
There are many who need
To know that God does care;
And can lift them from despair.

But how will they know;
Unless we go and show
God's love by how we live,
Unless we pray and give,
Unless we bear the cost,
Of reaching out to the lost?

Lord, give us a heart to care,
And a desire to share
Your love with those unseen,
In lands we've never been;
As in the sight of Jesus,
They are as precious as us.

⁷..... 'You must be born again.'
⁸The wind blows wherever it pleases .....
So it is with everyone born of the Spirit."
John 3:7,8

⁷the Lord God formed the man
from the dust of the ground,
and breathed into his nostrils
the breath of life,
and the man became a living being.
Genesis 2:7

The New Birth

We must be born again;
Allow the Spirit to reign,
Acknowledge Jesus as Lord,
To see the kingdom of God.

The Spirit purifies the soul,
Cleanses and makes it whole.
He is the Creator's breath,
The antidote for eternal death.

Like the wind that blows;
How it happens, no one knows.
But he is ever by our side,
To empower and to guide.

Lord, let your Wind blow,
Let your blessings flow,
For living is all in vain
Till we are born again.

55"Where, O death, is your victory?
Where, O death is your sting?"
57But thanks be to God!
He gives us the victory
through our Lord Jesus Christ.
1 Corinthians 15:55,57

There Is Life After Death

All is not over after final breath;
There is life after death!
Jesus will descend from the sky,
And in the twinkling of an eye,
There will be a great surprise,
For the dead in him shall rise.

Jesus has died and is risen!
Our sins have been forgiven.
Sin and death have no authority;
Christ has secured our victory.
Death and sin have no sting;
To him be praise and thanksgiving.

Death is no longer fatal
For God will make us immortal.
Our bodies will be imperishable,
Making everlasting life possible.
Watching and waiting will be over;
For we will be with God forever.

¹⁷" 'In the last days, God says,
I will pour out my Spirit on all people .....
¹⁹I will show wonders in the heaven above
and signs on the earth below .....
²¹And everyone who calls
on the name of the Lord will be saved.'
Acts 2:17,19,21

The Last Days

The Scriptures testify,
His people prophesy,
Signs and wonders appear,
The last days are here.

Jesus will come again
Forever to reign.
For he has secured victory
Over Satan's authority.

In God's new creation,
From every tribe and nation,
All who accept his salvation,
Will not incur condemnation.

Let us walk with God.
Let us preach his Word,
Lest at Jesus' reappearing
We are found wanting.

⁷"Ask and it will be given to you;
seek and you will find;
knock and the door will be opened to you.
Matthew 7:7

"You may ask me for anything
in my name, and I will do it.
John 14:14

³³ But seek first his kingdom
and his righteousness, ...
Matthew 6:33

²⁰ "Here I am!
I stand at the door and knock. .....
Revelation 3:20

ASK

Ask in Jesus' name;
He knows what is best.
Simply stake your claim
And he will do the rest.

Seek release from restlessness,
Worries, cares and strife.
God's kingdom and righteousness
Give abundant life.

Knock and if the door stays shut,
Perhaps you are not listening.
You could have locked Jesus out,
For he has been knocking.

Prayer is not a command
But a humble request.
God does not act as we demand;
He responds as he deems best.

³⁶Then Jesus went with his disciples
to a place called Gethsemane, ...
"Sit here while I go over there and pray."
³⁹..... "My Father, if it is possible,
may this cup be taken away from me.
Yet not as I will, but as you will."
Matthew 26:36,39

My Super Mobile Phone

I have a super mobile phone
That doesn't cost a cent.
It belongs to me alone
And cannot be lost or lent.

No tiresome battery charging,
No monthly subscriptions,
No costly model updating,
And the phone never malfunctions!

It's an excellent device
Linked to the highest Authority;
For comfort, help and advice
When I am in a quandary.

It has a dedicated line,
So calls don't have to wait.
It works wonderfully fine,
Especially when I am desperate.

I use my super phone everywhere;
There are no restrictions.
I simply lift my heart in prayer,
And God responds to my petitions.

¹Now faith is
being sure what we hope for
and certain of what we do not see.
⁸By faith Abraham,
when called to go .....obeyed .....
¹⁰For he was looking forward
to the city with foundations,
whose architect and builder is God.
Hebrews 11:1,8,10

Faith

Faith is the abiding certainty
Of God and hope of eternity.
It is not a wishful illusion,
Nor a mindless superstition.
For in creation and history
Is evidence of God's activity.

Faith is a life of adventure
With God into the future.
Stepping into the unknown
On his promises alone.
Obeying him absolutely
In prosperity and adversity.

Faith believes and pleases God
By acknowledging him as Lord.
It constantly looks forward,
To his promised reward
Of a wonderful celestial city;
Prepared for us in eternity.

16 "For God so loved the world
that he gave his one and only Son,
that whoever believes in him
shall not perish but have eternal life."
John 3:16

8 Love never fails. .....
13 And now these three remain:
faith, hope and love.
But the greatest of these is love.
1 Corinthians 13:8,13

Love

Jesus demonstrated God's love
By leaving his home above;
Exchanging his sovereignty
For a life of humility;
To serve and forgive,
And to die that we might live.

Love is more than empty speech,
Lofty ideals that we teach,
More than faith and prophecy,
Or understanding mystery,
More than the costly price
Of a martyr's sacrifice.

Love is not an outward show
Of how we feel or what we know.
It is a firm unfailing desire,
To serve, nourish and inspire,
Those who may cause us pain
With no thought of personal gain.

Love is thought, word and deed;
Touching lives of those in need.
It is not a natural inclination,
Or a shallow fleeting emotion;
But a virtue we can only afford
As a gift from a loving God.

27 "Peace I leave with you;
my peace I give you.
I do not give to you as the world gives.
Do not let your hearts be troubled
and do not be afraid.
John 14:27

33 ..... But take heart!
I have overcome the world."
John 16:33

Peace

We long for abiding peace,
For trouble and fear to cease;
But are helpless against strife
That engulf and stifle life.

Jesus lived with persecution;
Yet in the face of crucifixion
From which he had no release,
He promised us peace.

It was for us he had to die;
The wages of sin to satisfy.
Peace is to crown Jesus Lord,
And be reconciled to God.

Peace is not absence of strife;
But the presence of God in life
To conquer fear and adversity,
With confidence of victory.

Lord, help our striving cease.
Grant us your abiding peace,
Replace our restless anxiety
With your quiet serenity.

⁵For his anger lasts only a moment,
but his favour lasts a lifetime; …..
Psalm 30:5

¹¹"I have told you this
so that my joy may be in you
and that your joy may be complete."
John 15.11

Joy

We will encounter foes,
Life will have its woes.
But God will help us to survive;
Better still, he will give us life.

He will heal and he will save,
He will lift us from the grave.
Weeping may last through the night;
Joy comes with the Eternal Light.

For joy in all its fullness
Comes by abiding in Jesus.
By obeying God's commands;
Not doubting his demands.

It is not circumstances,
But God's love in Jesus,
We need always to deploy
To experience abiding joy.

[9] "The fear of the Lord is
the beginning of wisdom,
and knowledge of the Holy One
is understanding.
Proverbs 9:10

[5] If any of you lacks wisdom,
he should ask God, ...
and it will be given to him.
James 1:5

Wisdom

Wisdom surpasses knowledge,
For theories change with age.
Information floods the media,
Truth and falsehood are unclear.

Wisdom is to fear the Lord;
To live according to his word,
To discern truth from falsehood,
To forsake evil for good.

God gives wisdom liberally
To all who seek him earnestly
In times of doubt and need;
To avoid sin in thought and deed.

Lord and Master of my destiny;
You dictate how life should be.
Transform my mind anew
With wisdom to fear and love you.

²..... be transformed
by the renewing of your mind.
Then you will be able
to test and approve .....
his good, pleasing and perfect will.
Romans 12:2

⁵Your attitude should be
the same as that of Christ Jesus:
Philippians 2:5

Renewal Of The Mind

Lord, help us by your mercies,
To present our living bodies
A holy and acceptable sacrifice,
As our reasonable service.

Grant us a renewed mind
To leave worldly ways behind;
And accept, prove, and fulfill,
Your good and perfect will.

In a world of self and greed
That ignores those in need;
Teach us to think as Jesus thinks;
To love people and not things.

Make us channels of blessing
To the lost and suffering.
That as selfishness cease,
We may abide in your peace.

105Your word is a lamp to my feet
and a light for my path.
Psalm 119:105

11I have hidden your word in my heart
that I might not sin against you.
Psalm 119:11

18Open my eyes that I might see
wonderful things in your law.
Psalm 119:18

The Word Of God

Your word is a lamp to my feet,
Lighting up dangers that I meet.
Keeps me from going astray,
Every step along life's way.

Your word is a light to my path,
Guiding my journey on earth.
Directs my wandering soul
To your glorious eternal goal.

Your word I have kept in my heart,
That I may not sin and depart
From your just and righteous ways,
And to delight in you all my days.

Open my eyes that I may see
Your loving kindness and majesty;
To acknowledge you, Lord,
As my Creator and my God.

Extracts Of Selected Reviews

Christian Literature offers a wonderful medium for sharing God's love. It transcends time and personal boundaries, articulates truths we have difficulty expressing, and speaks to the reader when he is most receptive. Extracts of reviews from some readers are featured below.

Written in a light and casual style, *Time Belongs To God And Other Poems* takes passages from the Bible and paints scenes of challenges we constantly encounter to provoke a deeper appreciation of God's love and faithfulness. Using contemporary problems of greed, injustice and wickedness, each poem moves the reader from an abstract to a more positive understanding of God and how by allowing him to work in and through us, we can transform the world for better.

Each poem leaves the reader with a desire, a prayer and promise for greater awareness of God at work in his life. Reading a poem in the morning and at night has helped to make my burdens lighter as it reminds me of God's abiding power and love.

Mr Chiang Ming Cherng

I had great consolation reading the book of poetry *Time Belongs To God And Other Poems*. It expresses what I know but cannot define, how I feel but cannot express. I have bought copies to give to relatives and friends.

Mrs Tan Siok Eng

By blending Scripture with poetry, Kwok Thye has given weight to this timely collection; an enjoyable resource for spiritual reflection.

Dr Clarence Tan

It was not easy to share the Christian Faith with my stepbrother who was terminally with cancer. *Time Belongs To God And Other Poems* came in very handy. The poem *Soaring On Eagles' Wings* was particularly helpful. My stepbrother received Christ into his life and is now home with the Lord. Praise God.

Mrs Eilleen Chia

Time Belongs To God And Other Poems reminds us of the challenges we face as we journey on this earth. However, we are greatly encouraged; God is always with us – till eternity, if only we worship and love Him as the one true God. Kwok Thye has been blessed with a wonderful way with words and writes meaningful poetry. I trust it will bring you joy, comfort and strength as it has done for me.

Dr Mavis Yeo

Kwok Thye in expressing the truth of Scripture in poetry has helped us to experience God's teaching in righteousness (2 Tim. 3:16 & 17) more easily as poetry has a way of speaking to the "mind, soul and spirit" of a person directly and personally, thereby building up the person in his or her faith in, and discipleship of, Jesus Christ.

I thank God for *Time Belongs To God And Other Poems* and I recommend any Christian wanting an "easy–to-carry around" booklet for devotional and ministry use and reflection, and to have copies for sharing with others who are wanting to know more of God and His loving ways.

Rev Kenneth Huang

About the Author

The author is a Chartered Civil Engineer. He developed a passion for Bible study and Christian literature during his student days in Australia through the Overseas Christian Fellowship, a student movement affiliated to the Inter-Varsity Fellowship.

He continued this passion on his return to Singapore through Scripture Union, the Christian Book Centre, and the Bible Study Fellowship. He has also been involved in facilitating development of Bible study groups for adults and pastoral care ministries for students. He reads widely for leisure and to keep abreast of current affairs.

Printed in the United States
By Bookmasters